Shops Remembered and Walmer

Mrs Betty Rogers behind the counter of her bakery c1950.

Bygone Publishing

Front cover shows John Rogers, with daughters Eileen and Maureen, outside his shop at 132 High Street, Deal, during the 1930s.

Contents

For Charles with love and thanks for all his help and support.
And in memory of Uncle John Gaunt who ignited my interest in local history.

Introduction

The idea for this book grew from my research in the East Kent Mercury newspaper each week for its On File column. So often the snippets of news evoked a picture of the working lives and struggles of Deal and Walmer's local traders.

One early memorable item from 1906 described 'a horse attached to a van belonging to Donovan's Hand Laundry became a little restive on Saturday morning and the cover of the van tore the sun blind in front of Mr HG Frost's shop.'

Later, the arrival of the car led to numerous street widening schemes which demolished businesses – as did Second World War bomb damage.

The 'credit crunch' of 2008 and 2009, increased car parking charges and business rate rises all contributed to a spate of shop closures. I did not expect to record the demise of Woolworth's, Walter & Son, Curry's, Brown and Phillips' or Laughton's but their closure reinforced the urgency of documenting all the businesses under threat and celebrating those that had gone before.

The sequence of photos can be followed for a walk around the town, starting in Beach Street to Alfred Square, Middle Street to Broad Street and Queen Street into West Street, Western Road. After the length of the High Street the sequence moves to Victoria Road, The Strand, Dover Road and then takes in Mill Hill before ending with a look at some of the corner shops around Deal and Walmer.

Judith Gaunt
Deal
October 2009

Acknowledgements

I would like to thank Charles Finn, Peter Latham, Val Mercer, Martin Tapsell and Marion Walsh for taking the contemporary photographs that appear in this book.

I am indebted to my cousin Gloria Pellatt for the generous use of the local history photographic collection of her father, the late John Gaunt. I must also thank Nick Kidd for offering me the opportunity to choose and reproduce photographs taken by the late Basil Kidd.

I would also like to thank the following for allowing me to reproduce their photographs: Diane Almond, Mr Wilfred Almond, Jim Ashby, Johnny Beerling, EH Brown, Jane Brown, Mrs Janet Chandler, Mrs Georgina Childs, Mrs Vera Clarke, Mr Richard Coe, Georgina Curling, Bill Dawkins, Elizabeth Densham, Mary Guiver, Mrs Joan Harlow, Mrs Christine Haswell, Mrs Cecily Hearn, Gregory Holyoake, Andy Horne, Mrs Audrey Johnson, Sir Wayne King, Bryn and Julie Limbrick, Tony May, Mrs Valerie Oatridge, Nicola Orchard, Herbert Piddock, Cdr John Prime RN, Jenny Rawlinson, Mrs Christine Rayner, Cherry Robinson, Mr John Rogers and the late Mrs Betty Rogers, Mrs Dot and Claire Sansum, Andrew Sargent, Susan Solley, June Spinner, Molly Staples, Mrs Sarah Strachan, Bob Strouts, Peter Sullivan, Dr J Tapping, Mr Keith Tapping, Eileen Wagstaff, John Ward, Frankie Wellard, the Wilson family, Marion Wood, Alan Yates, Paula Young.

The following organisations have been generous in giving permission for their photographs to be reproduced: Bright and Bright Estate Agents, Country Life magazine, Deal and Walmer Chamber of Trade, Deal Library, Deal Town Council, Dover District Council, Dover Museum, Graham Smith, editor East Kent Mercury, English Heritage, Francis Frith & Co, Kent County Council Strategy and Planning Directorate, VDBM Chartered Surveyors.

I must also thank the following for their help, especially Julie Deller for reading through my draft, offering information and support. Also: Mrs Margaret Ablett and the former staff of Walter & Son, Deal, Bill and Sue Ashby, Vicky Barnsley, Sue Briggs, Edwin Brown, Les Cory, Bert and Georgina Curling, Deal Library staff especially Denise Coe and Sarah Frampton, Deal Local History and Maritime Museum, Diana Ferrell and former staff of Woolworth's, Deal, Mark Frost Dover Museum, Steve Glover, A Harris, Gregory Holyoake, John Howland, Mrs J Moseling, Susan Newing, Mrs Shirley Norris, Mrs Valerie Oatridge, Michael Rogers, Bill Startup, Martin Tapsell and Doreen Turner.

And finally many thanks to my publisher Nick Evans of Bygone Publishing for his patience and support in editing and producing this book and for allowing me to reproduce photographs from the collection of his late father, Bill Evans.

Beach Street – Some of Deal's early traders set up shop on the seafront in dangerous times to take advantage of the naval and sea trade. In 1643 William Mathews, a linen draper, was prosecuted by the captain of Deal Castle for trading too close to the sea, 'blocking the line of sight and hindering the plying of ordnance'. Mathews complained saying he had bought a shop for £50 near the King's Head and wanted a licence to cover in the building, which was granted.

BEACH STREET, DEAL.

Edwin Fredrick Giraud owned the fancy goods and bookshop that later became FH Whittingham's surplus clothing store in the 1950s. On the left is Mangilli's Grand Café and Restaurant run by Achille Mangilli from the late 1890s and then by Tobia Mangilli until the 1930s. It later became The Pegasus Café, popular for egg and chips on a Saturday night. Ian Dunkerley purchased the cafe in 1987 and extended into The Pier Hotel 10 years later.

The Promenade, Deal

On the left at 27 Beach Street was Foad's Creamery, owned by Walter James Foad. Later it became a branch of RG Waters dairy. Without fridges, people needed local dairies to supply milk and cream products and Waters had dairy herds at Walmer Court and Clarence Farms. For many years the property was the Corner Parlour run by Mr and Mrs B Davies.

Left: One of the last remaining shops along Beach Street was the Foc'sle fishing tackle shop which closed in 2007. Pete and Pat Young owned the shop for 25 years after taking it over from Mr and Mrs C Hurd. Around 1896 the property had been Lloyd's Signal station, handling communications for Lloyd's of London. One of the earlier shopkeepers here was grocer James Fitch.

Above: Pete Young with a Thornback Ray he caught fishing over the Goodwin Sands from a Deal boat. He and his wife Pat both sadly died in 2007.

Numbers 37 to 39 Beach Street before they became part of The Quarterdeck site. Number 37 shows the business of William Loften Brook, 'fly proprietor' and lodging house as well as confectioner and tobacconist from around 1899. By 1913 Alfred Ernest Rose was trading as a tailor at the premises and by 1959 it was a hat shop. Number 39 was John Thomas Outwin's newsagent, later run by Charles Thierens.

Numbers 43 and 45 Beach Street were the bakery and restaurant business of William Oatridge and later Gordon Blain. The premises were alongside The Antwerp Hotel, now The Bohemian, and directly opposite Deal Pier. The buildings suffered bomb damage during the Second World War and were later demolished to form part of The Quarterdeck site.

William Oatridge with his delivery van parked at the Court Road and Station Road junction.

PHONE DEAL 100

GORDON BLAIN

HIGH-CLASS
FAMILY AND COMMERCIAL
HOTEL

CAFE
RESTAURANT AND
BANQUETING HALL

Directly Opposite the Pier

The art deco lines of Gordon Blain's fruit shop that sat alongside the restaurant and bakery on the seafront. Gordon was a London baker who visited Deal for the fishing. By 1930 he had purchased Oatridge's. He had a second shop at 92 High Street which was bombed during World War Two. By the time he died in 1938, Gordon owned 100 shops in London and Essex as well as farms in Mongeham and Essex. Inset: A 1931 advert for Blain's Deal store.

A view of Beach Street around 1860. To the extreme right at number 72 was Royal House. Mr James King's toy shop and Mr and Mrs Whaley's stationers and newspaper reading rooms were in the property with the unusual blinds in the centre of this photo. It became Dudley House and subsequently Deal Beach Parlour. Further along was Mr William Fells, tailor, taken over by Mr John Burns, later becoming part of Dolmar at number 61. Inset: A Dolmar advert from 1956. The ladies' wear shop and the antique shop next door were owned by Mr and Mrs C Sage.

A closer view of Royal House which was demolished for road widening and now the site of the Royal Hotel car park. The house was once the baker and confectionery shop of Richard Fox & Son and later the furniture and antique shop of Messrs Dean Corke & Sons. Just beyond was Mr W Groombridge's tobacconist and confectioner. Right: A ceramic lid for a cold cream pot prepared by WH Humfrey, a chemist in the late 1890s set on the corner of Beach Street and King Street. Later it was run by Mr C Harbron and then became Lewis the Chemist before becoming The Caterer.

Prepared by
COLD
CREAM
W·H·HUMFREY, Chemist, PIER PARADE, DEAL.

This row of properties has seen a variety of businesses over the centuries. The Lobster Pot café was at 81-83 Beach Street; number 81 had been Stephen Brittenden's bakery from the late 1800s, later TJ Griffin confectioner. At 83 was George Milton's greengrocers, later run by Cecil Goymer. At number 85 at the start of the 1900s was The Creamery run by Mrs Bampling. Divito's ice cream parlour, on the corner of Oak Street, had been Henry Larkin's fishmongers.

Just beyond the row of shops in the previous illustration, before Oak Street, was a butcher's shop owned by Agnes Jennings. The building is believed to have been bombed during the Second World War. The vertically, or horizontally, opening windows were a familiar feature of shops selling perishable goods. At 91 Beach Street was the Wedgewood Dairy run by RS Newbury.

J MacDonald, newsagent, stationer and tobacconist shop at 151 Beach Street next door to The Pelican public house pictured around 1950. Inset: John 'Mac' MacDonald and his wife Lillian shortly before their retirement. They had run the newsagent since 1933. By 1959 when they celebrated their diamond wedding anniversary Mac, then aged 80, still cycled around the town three times a day delivering newspapers. He had been born in Gibraltar and grew up in London.

BEACH STREET, DEAL.

An earlier view of the newsagent and tobacconist shop, seen to the extreme right alongside The Pelican public house in 1921. Standing in the doorway is possibly Robert Bussey, the owner around this period.

An even earlier view of Beach Street with The Pelican public house roughly centre. Opposite was the walled building of the Pilot House. Its wooden landing stage, which led to the sea, can just be seen behind it.

A view along Beach Street, looking back towards the Royal Hotel, captured by Country Life magazine for its August 1947 issue which discussed controversial plans to demolish part of the conservation area. TF Pain & Son's street directory for 1948 lists the corner shop at 179 Beach Street as St Margaret's Café owned by Mrs S Swift. An earlier directory for 1922 had HJT Watkins in business here as a boot and shoe repairer.

Alfred Square – Former residents of Alfred Square remember it being 'like a village' with a good variety of shops. On the left at number 3, in this contemporary view, was E Smith and Son fish shop from around 1910 to 1937, selling wet and cured fish and became one of the town's first fish and chip shops. At number 7 was a grocery shop run by Edward Sprattling, later owned by George William Rayworth around 1911 and followed by Mr and Mrs Wilson.

Edward Samuel Smith and his family selling fresh and cured fish from their home in Brewer Street around 1900, as did his father John before him. Edward later set up E Smith and Son's fish shop at 3 Alfred Square.

An older Edward joking with the camera, with wife Selina in the doorway of their fish shop at 3 Alfred Square. The doorway was later moved to the side of the building. They are pictured with their friend Louie, right, on the steps next door.

Preparations for a charabanc outing in Alfred Square around 1920. To the left is the coal merchant business of Thomas Henry Williams. His wife Mary Ann ran a grocery shop in the front room, entered from the side of the property in Alfred Row. The sign for E Smith and Son fishmongers can be seen next door. To the far right at the top of the square was the sweet shop and general store of William John Thomas at 164 Middle Street.

R. REDSULL,

FAMILY BUTCHER,

9, ALFRED SQUARE, DEAL.

Best Canterbury Lamb and Mutton. —

— Prime American Beef.

HOME-KILLED PORK AND VEAL.

At the top of Alfred Square at the corner of Sandown Road was Robert Redsull's butchers shop, later run by his son Cecil Bernard Redsull. Cecil's daughter remembers huge ice blocks being delivered by lorry and carried down to the cellar to keep the meat chilled before refrigeration was widely available. Inset left: Cecil Redsull taken in the late 1940s or early 1950s. Inset: An R Redsull advertisement from 1911.

A contemporary view of Alfred Square looking towards Cavendish House, on the left and on the corner of North Street, which was a bakery for centuries and for many years run by John and Betty Rogers. On the right of the picture, at 164 Middle Street, now a private house, was WT Thomas's general store and sweet shop.

Cavendish House at the top of Alfred Square, and technically 1 North Street, was a bakery from at least 1851. The 34 year old baker was William Silth who lived on the premises with his sister and two assistants, Thomas Coons and John Kemp. The shop was later run by Mrs Sarah Andrews in the 1930s and taken on by John and Betty Rogers in 1947.

Mrs Betty Rogers behind the counter at Cavendish House. Betty came from Wales and met her husband John while he was stationed there during the Second World War. Mr Rogers had worked for Cavell's bakery in Upper Queen Street after leaving school in 1931. The couple set up their business in 1947 and they later opened Church Path Bakery on the corner of Albert Road. Sadly, Betty died in April 2009.

In this view of the Caxton Home, now Lloyd Court, which occupied one side of Alfred Square, were to the left, 'Georgie' Bishop's barber shop and North Deal Wool Shop owned by Mrs Town. Mrs Smith stands at 13 Alfred Square in her long white apron. She sold wet fish during the day and fish and chips at night. Further down, Newing & Co's paraffin and general store, Flynn's fruit shop and Ernest Voizey's butchers, on the corner, were all bombed during the Second World War when several people were killed.

Middle Street – Former residents also remember Middle Street as a village, once again with shops for all their needs. Some former shops retain their features but number 154, on the left, no longer does. This property had a doorway at the front with shutters that were taken down when the shop was open. Mr and Mrs Pollington ran the business in the 1950s.

An older view of Griffin Street looking towards Middle Street. On the left of the picture, at 155, was a corner shop with a Dutch gable end feature. The grocer's shop was run by Thomas Shibberfield and his wife Ann around 1850 and generations of shopkeepers followed including FE Wythe in the 1950s. The shop entrance has since been bricked up, no doubt to prevent the weather blowing in from the sea!

Lower down Griffin Street was the bakery of William George Goldfinch. Customers entered the shop by the alleyway on the right hand side of the premises. History has it that special ships' biscuits were cooked here for Nelson's men and the Duke of Wellington was a customer. Right, is a modern view of Goldfinch & Son who ran the business for more than 120 years. By 1959 the business was owned by EJ Spray.

Number 128 Middle Street, on the corner of Golden Street, was Josephine's Tearooms for many years. In the 1930s it had been known as Granny Smith's corner shop but became Marchant's general grocery store during the 1950 and 1960s.

A view today along Middle Street showing number 98 just before the junction with Coppin Street. In this short space there were several shops but although some retain their features, none remain in business.

A further view of 98 Middle Street at the corner of Coppin Street from 1934. On the opposite corner at 96 Middle Street was Richard Roberts butcher and at 94, John William Drew was shopkeeper. John Drew Junior was also enterprising, advertising his chimney and window cleaning business (carpets beaten) from the premises.

Left: The corner shop at 98 Middle Street when used as the fishing tackle and gun shop of TR Franks. Previously, the building had been Ye Olde Grocery Stores, right, at 98 Middle Street, on the corner of Coppin Street, notable for its fine curved upper window. The shop was run by John Turton around 1934 and earlier Charles and Elizabeth Ann Stubberfield served the local customers.

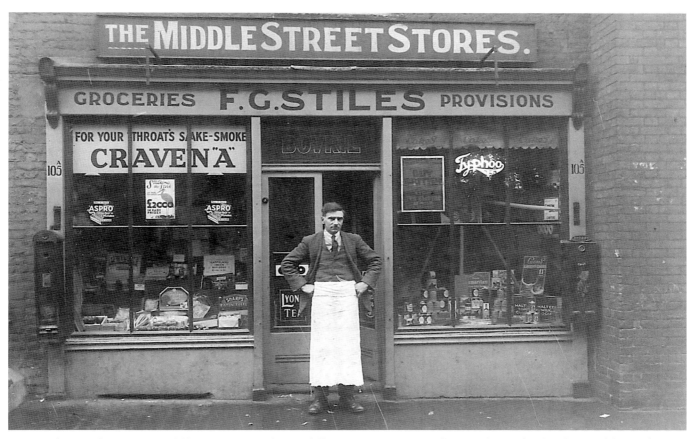

Across the road at 105a Middle Street was the Middle Street Stores run by Frank Gayford Stiles and his wife Arondie in the 1930s and early 1940s. They left Deal for Wales during the Second World War. The shop was later run by WA Casson. Note the advert for Craven A cigarettes, said to prevent sore throats!

Number 108 Middle Street, on the corner of Farrier Street, happily still retains its shop features albeit altered slightly. Mrs S Crews ran her small grocery store here with her daughter during the 1950s and 1960s. A blind keeps the sun from the produce in the windows. Note the bubble gum vending machine on the wall and the advertising signs for two leading brands of tea.

Going back further in time from the previous picture, Percy Clark ran his bakery at 108 Middle Street from the late 1800s. Next door but one at 106 is pictured George Roberts outside his secondhand shop which his family had earlier run as a grocery store.

There were dozens of local shops to serve their customers but these stores needed goods to sell.
Right: CR Marsh, wholesale grocer, was based at 77 Middle Street and supplied many shops in the town and neighbouring villages. Just beyond the premises is the shop on the corner of St George's Passage.
Top left: John Ward pictured, driver for CR Marsh, in 1937 filling the Morris Commercial delivery van with petrol at Old's Garage in West Street. Below left: A full view of the vehicle reveals CR Marsh was established in 1889.

Ian Loughran outside his shop Vivaldi's Fine China on the corner of Middle Street and St George's Passage. He opened the business in 1998 and closed on retirement in December 2008. The corner property reopened as Sara's Chocolates, keeping going a tradition of shops in Middle Street. Earlier, it had been a branch of Jesse Springett Huntley, antique furniture dealers.

A. W. BAILEY,

HIGH-CLASS BUTCHER.

Southdown House, 14, King Street, Deal.

Elms Vale Laundry, on the corner of King Street and Middle Street closed in 2008. This corner property, called Southdown House, was earlier AW Bailey butcher and previously The Central Meat Store, owned by H Jennings butcher. At one time it was also the town's Post Office. Inset: An advertisement for Bailey's the butcher from 1938.

This view is a reminder that many quaint buildings and alleyways were lost to the creation of Middle Street car park. On the corner of Custom House Lane at 44 Middle Street was William Croft's pork butchers, bombed during the Second World War. The view is taken from the side of A Simmond's Jeweller at 60 High Street. In the foreground is the watercress barrow of John Williams, of Custom House Lane, who sold his produce in Park Street, including violets in season, moving his barrow on when the local policeman came into view!

On the left is the corner of Custom House Lane and Croft's butchers, shown in the previous picture. Further along at 40 and 42 Middle Street, and now also part of the car park, was Gray and Weston outfitters which stands derelict and damaged from bomb blast. Previously CB Wellden ran his drapery business at the premises, which he established in 1817. Sadly, attempts to save the Georgian house in the picture failed and it was demolished.

Left: Mr Bill Smith, who had a firewood shop on the corner of Middle Street and Custom House Lane. In his arms is son Bill. Bill senior was the brother of Edwin Samuel Smith, fishmonger of 3 Alfred Square. Right: A lost view of Middle Street, from behind Deal library. To the left is Harris Mayes butcher's van with the slogan 'Deal's leading butcher'. Their other slogan 'Deal with Mayes, it pays' is on the building behind. The firm's slaughterhouse was in the Coach Yard, behind their shop at 44 High Street. On the right is Alfred Beeston's grocery store at 28 Middle Street.

Broad Street – John Rayner celebrates with his staff in the 1970s on winning yet another prize for a shop window display. Mr Rayner had been manager of Pilcher and Chittenden's greengrocers in the High Street, on the corner of Park Street, but later set up on his own with his Broad Street and High Street shops.

Queen Street – Edward Methold's grocery shop was on the corner of High Street and Queen Street but was demolished as part of Queen Street road widening. In 1923 Boots the chemist was built on the site. Later, Boots moved to its current position and the shop became a branch of Lilley & Skinner shoe shops. In more recent times, it became Mansfield's shoe shop, the Northern Rock Building Society and Select boutique.

A closer view of the properties demolished for road widening at the lower end of Queen Street, looking towards Broad Street. They included Mr E Williams' saddle and harness shop and Mr Harry Frank Romney's bakers and confectioners.

A view looking back up Queen Street; centre is Spencer Smith's butchers which became CE Thorpe's butchers. To the left was HS Thacker's dairy, later RG Water's dairy, then EF Howe stationers; AW Page's shoe shop, later RT Kelway's shoe shop and now Halifax estate agents. Next came Vye & Son, the grocer's Queen Street branch.

C. E. THORPE,

Late SPENCER SMITH,

FAMILY BUTCHER,

Purveyor of Finest
English Meat only.

———

2, QUEEN STREET, DEAL.

Telephone DEAL 107.

Above: An advertisement for Thorpe's butchers in Queen Street.

Left: Mr Bob Thorpe, butcher, with his wife Ivy, son Ronald and daughter Peggy.

On the left, the one time JobCentre, was Dobson's Café later Little's Café. Brown and Phillips leased the property and in 1957 part of it became the 'Young-set shop, a new shop for fashion conscious teenagers and twenties'. Across the road more of the shops were demolished for road widening, including Mr Inkerman Baker's ham and beef stores.

Staff of Vye's 'the Kentish grocer' outside the branch at 10 Queen Street c1949. They include Mr Capell, manager, Mr Hayward, Bill Wratton, Mr Long, Betty Finnis, Mr Fuller, John Winwood, June Saunders, Ena Cavell and Betty Holiday. Inset: An advertisement for Vye's from 1933.

An earlier photocall for Vye's Queen Street staff, possibly from the late 1920s; the shop is lit by gas light. Staff had entered into the spirit to promote a shopping week gala held from 5th to 10th December. The photograph was taken by CH Lawrence of 1 Griffin Street.

The Odeon cinema stands in all its art deco splendour, photographed by John Maltby in 1936 as part of his commission to record every Odeon in the country. The picture was taken as Charles Laughton featured in Mutiny On The Bounty. The shops beside it were erected on the former Admiralty House site. Evelyn's florist became Mead's china and gift shop and then Joyce Heath's china shop before she moved to Deal High Street. Mrs E Chandler's gown shop was alongside and later on, the Pearl wallpaper shop traded in this row.

A view of Upper Queen Street, as it was earlier called, near the entrance to Deal railway station. The houses in the centre of the photograph were demolished to widen the station approach. In the foreground is The White Horse Hotel, again demolished for road widening. Between, at 2 Upper Queen Street, was Frederick Ewell's grocer, later becoming Charles Weston's grocers and at number 3 was a branch of Cavell's bakery.

West Street – Judging by the rolls of lino on display, this photo of Job's of Deal was taken in the 1980s. It was well known for decades before demolition in 1996 to form part of Sainsbury's supermarket car park. Stapleton Willey Job began the firm in West Street in the late 1890s. His son, Cedric, and grandson Maurice, carried on the business until its closure. In earlier days Job's hired out prams and wheelchairs to the town's tourists from its children's department as well as selling furniture and household items.

Left: A young Zena Almond working in the Land Army during the Second World War at Clarke's Nursery, now called Walmer Nurseries, in Dover Road. Right: Miss Almond ran Zena's florist in a small shop on the corner of Century Walk and West Street in the 1950s, again demolished for road widening. It had previously been 'Angel' Gabriel's barber and tobacconist.

West Street Cycles was at 92 West Street and, although long closed, retains some of its shop features. During the Second World War a wireless set was tuned to the news in the lean-to shed section on the left of this view. People from nearby gathered to hear the latest broadcasts as battery wireless sets were not in every home. In 1979 Ted and Dot Boreham took over from Mr Box.

Above: A young Jane Brown stands in front of her father Fred's butchers shop in Western Road alongside their home at Walmer Villa sometime in the mid 1950s. The extension, built by her grandfather who had a shop at 31 College Road, is now RAM computers.

Right: Alfred George Brown is pictured with his assistants at his butchers shop at 31 College Road. Mr Brown purchased the pork butcher and greengrocers for £30 from William Neeve in 1907. Today's health and safety inspectors would not appreciate the meat displays nor the young boy sat on the carcass of a pig in the foreground.

High Street – The houses in this photograph are at the far end of the High Street just past Alfred Square. The second house, number 199, is just before the junction with Water Street and is now a private property. The house no longer retains any external shop features but was JH Staley's greengrocers shop. Alongside it had been a branch of RG Water's dairy.

Once again 'demolished for road widening' is the phrase to explain the sad loss, in the late 1950s of a row of buildings including the general draper's shop at 193 High Street, on the corner of Water Street. The premises had been owned by William James Curtis and by 1930 had been taken over by Charles E Daggett. The picture is a reminder of just how vibrant the north end of Deal High Street was with its wealth and variety of shops.

At Kent House 188, 190 and 192 High Street was Edward Samuel Smith general grocer. He was known as 'Teddy Midnight' for his long opening hours and was creative and forceful in his advertisements 'No overweight, no bonus, no dividend, no bribery. We do not charge 1/6d for our 1/4d tea to give you back 2d. Everything at rock bottom prices.' Inset: The original shop sign was exposed for a time during alterations to the building in 2008.

One of the most affectionately remembered businesses in the town was the Dustpan Stores at 182-186 High Street on the corner of Griffin Street. It was opened in 1867 as HWR Thompson and Sons. The shop got its nickname owing to the large dustpan structure fixed on the roof surrounded by red, white and blue light bulbs during the Christmas season.

Seed merchants T Denne and Sons occupied distinctive premises for many years until becoming the Multilines discount store. That business in turn gave way to Channel Wines which traded from the building until 2008. On the far side of The Old Forge is RT Baker's shoe shop, established in 1837. It closed in 1985 when the third generation owner, Mr Jeffrey Baker, retired.

This view includes The Old Forge and RT Baker's shoe shop on the left shown in the previous photo. On the right is the row of shops and private houses demolished for road widening and now form part of the Union Road car park. On the extreme right is 155 High Street with a sign for 'New Look Homes' selling 'contemporary wallpaper'. It had earlier been E Cohen's outfitter in the 1920s and 1930s. GA Stupples' fish and chip shop was also in this row at number 151.

The vacant showroom of Parkin's Garage is in the foreground while Cleveland petrol pumps can be glimpsed through the windows. The premises were formerly Crump's Garage, on the corner of Union Road and now part of the car park. Earlier they had been Crump's Dining Rooms and in the late 1800s the Victorian Restaurant. The Congregational Church, now the Landmark Centre, looks imposing with its twin spires known as Inspire and Aspire.

HIGH STREET, DEAL.

This is the High Street decorated for the coronation of George V on 22 June 1911. On the left, at 143, was Crump's Dining Rooms, formerly the Victoria Restaurant run by Alfred Cowles. Beyond was the garage and Queen's Arms public house – all demolished for road widening. On the right were WJ Smith's hairdresser while RE King's tobacconist marked the turning into Farrier Street.

Right: Robert Ebenezer King was a tobacconist at 146 High Street, when tobacco advertising was celebrated. Robert was the father of Sir Alex King of King's Bazaar toy shop. The tobacconist's premises, now alongside Hooper's Interiors, was called Snuff, Puff and Candy in the 1960s and 1970s and, although closed, still retains a cigarette machine outside the premises as a reminder of its former use.

Below: A small plate under the coin slot tells us three 10p coins were all that was required to buy 10 Cadets or Senior Service when the machine was last used, possibly in the early 1980s.

A view of the High Street in 1957; the Wall's ice cream sign of Japp's sweet shop showing on the left. On the right, the shops included D Bradshaw's butchers, the World Stores and Mr Moffatt the tailor in what had previously been the World Store's off licence – both now form the Hospice Shop. Newing's cycle shop and showroom were at 138 and 140. Inset: An advert for the cycle shop, first opened by Ernest Duncan Newing in 1909. His son John, took over in 1924 aged only 15, when Ernest died. The shop is now Carried Away.

On the retirement of John Newing in 1970, Newing's cycle shop at 140 High Street became a fruiterer and greengrocer run by John Rayner who already had a greengrocers in Broad Street. He later changed the High Street store into a Christian bookshop having decided there was a need for such a business – it is now Deal Christian Resource Centre.

Bill Maxted's pet shop at 134 High Street was previously Mr E Potter's fishmonger. The pet shop was taken over by Bill's niece and husband, Patrick and Marianne McNicholas in 1981; Marianne was Mayor of Deal in 1989. They moved the business next door into number 136 within the year to what had been Gabriel's Café, often called 'Papa Gabriel's' or 'Gabs,' an establishment many people have said they weren't allowed in by their parents – but went anyway.

Currently Delpierre Antiques, 132 High Street was the general store of John 'Jack' Thomas Rogers. He was born in Deal in 1886 and after service in the army returned to open his shop in the early 1930s. Jack stands with his daughters Eileen, left, and Maureen. Note the signs for Deal rock at 1d and 3d each. Regular customers could also contribute to a fireworks club. Later, the premises became Hutton's dairy shop run by Doris Carpenter.

Left: George Noble and daughter Emma in the doorway of their leather shop at 102 High Street. The property was later incorporated into Stewart Dunn's chemist shop which was established in 1885 and had a large photographic and processing department. The property is now a newsagent.

Below: A 1957 advert for Stewart Dunn and Son, from the town guide of the same year.

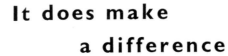

In October 1942 a bomb destroyed Gordon Blain's fruiterer and bakery at 92 and 92a High Street, opposite the Rose Hotel, damaging Percy Comfort's ironmongers and King's Bazaar across at St George's Passage. Martin's jewellers was damaged trapping Mrs Martin for several hours. The landmark cupola on this site, which could formerly be seen from the opposite end of the High Street, was destroyed in the bombing.

Pictured during the 1930s, King's toy and fancy goods shop stood at 88 High Street, opposite The Rose Hotel and St George's church. After the building was bombed in 1942, it relocated to 1 High Street at the corner of Wellington Road. Alongside is a glimpse of JW Cox the chemist's shop, previously run by George Head and earlier Tyson Stubbs, and now Season's cafe.

Every child's dream, and perhaps dad's as well, a shop full of Meccano and Hornby train sets. This later view of King's Bazaar at 88 High Street, opposite The Rose Hotel, was taken before the property was damaged, and later demolished, owing to Second World War bombing. The firm moved to the corner of Wellington Road at 1 King Street and continued to be a mecca for local children.

Frederick Lass, pastry cook and confectioner, traded from 1828 at 84 High Street, now Swanstitch. It later became Gammage's. Tea, coffee and chocolate drinks were available, while wedding cakes were a speciality. The entrance was then at the side, with a deep step down into it and a second inside, recalling the High Street's earlier name as Lower Street.

Below: Takeaways are nothing new. A pastry dish from F Lass, 'Please return this dish' it implores.

Laughton's, originally Baldwin's, moved from these premises in December 2008 to a smaller store at the rear of HSBC bank. Thanet born Theophilus Collins Baldwin opened his drapery and millinery store at 74 High Street in 1874, later extending to numbers 76 and 78, creating a large and prosperous business. The store later became Avora and then Superdeal before becoming Laughton's and is now a branch of The Original Factory Shop.

High Street, Deal

At the centre of this 1930 scene is Baldwin's when shopping streets were bedecked with sunblinds. Further down can be seen WR Turk's jewellers and clockmakers as well as the cupola above the row of shops that was bombed during the Second World War. On the right of the view is Hunnisett's drapers at 70 and 72 High Street that was Deal's original Town Hall. In 1959, when this shop became Baldwin's bedding department, the firm applied for, but was refused, permission to extend across the opening to Market Street. Later Joyce Heath moved her china shop here from Queen Street. Inset: A Hunnisett's receipt for goods purchased in June 1953.

Above: A scene from a Baldwin's staff party in 1962, held in the function room above Catt's Restaurant in Market Street. Many shops employed far more staff than today, often with two or more at each counter to serve customers. In the foreground at the end of the table on the left is Miss Harris, with Miss Hoare to her right. On the extreme right of the picture is Miss Sandys.

Right: Mr Wilfred Barber, director and manager of the Deal store from 1947, with his wife Doris. By this time, Baldwin's was part of a group of 28 shops which included Lewis and Hyland's Kent department stores and a shirt factory.

White Fuller (Kent) Limited on the corner of High Street and King Street is now Bigg's opticians. Cecil Charles Prime and Frank Dobell bought out Mr White and Mr Fuller in the 1930s and ran the branches in Deal, Ramsgate, Margate and later Sandwich.

Below: Cecil William Lamond Prime, who took over from his father, with his familiar buttonhole.

The quintessential shop fittings of earlier times captured in this internal view, possibly dating from the early 1960s, of White Fuller (Kent) Limited. The shop supplied the uniforms for a number of schools in the area including Sir Roger Manwood's at Sandwich, whose striped crest can be seen beside the assistant on the left of the picture. Inset: Staff stand proudly outside the premises, the windows decorated for Christmas sometime in the 1970s.

High Street   Deal

Deal High Street before the junction with Park Street c1910. On the left is a glimpse of Brown's drapers, which became Brown and Phillips; the boys in gowns and mortar boards are possibly from Deal College, now Lloyd Court. To the right, Freeman, Hardy and Willis's shoe shop, now Zoom Photos, displays its row of gas lamps. On the corner opposite was Giraud's bookshop and library which later became a branch of Lipton's grocers.

A Victorian view of Deal High Street from the corner of Park Street showing the variety and style of shop frontages. Giraud's stationers and stamp office included 'Deal Library in association with Mudies'. Charles Edward Mudie was a publisher who created a lending service throughout the country. Immediately beyond, with impressive gas lamps, was John Pittock's drapers and outfitters. Opposite, were George Mence Smith general stores and Henry Frost's ironmongers.

In the 1950s, Maypole Dairy, at 67 High Street, was part of a large chain comprising Pearks, Home & Colonial and Lipton's. Various takeovers would see these names swallowed up. Alongside was Freeman, Hardy & Willis's shoe shop and, set back, was Pilcher & Chittenden's fruit shop, now the Halifax Building Society. Across the road was Brown & Phillips while Bata's shoe shop was next door at number 62 on the corner of Custom House Lane.

z

q

Lipton's grocery shop stands on the corner of Park Street, which had earlier been Giraud's stationers. Lipton's later moved to 8-10 High Street, now Superdrug, in the 1970s, a larger self service store. Alongside Lipton's is Gieves and Hawkes which opened in John Pittock's outfitters on the retirement of Mr Pittock in 1978. The updated frontage of the Co-op store was next along – that became Seeboard's electricity showroom, then Curry's and now WH Smith. This 1983 view shows no entry signs denoting the first stages of pedestrianisation.

Photographed at sometime in the 1960s are staff from Bata's shoe shop which was found at 62 High Street on the corner of Custom House Lane. From left are an unknown temporary manager, Christine Burton, Molly Weller, now Staples, and Dawn Buddle. The Bata chain was founded in 1894, in what is now the Czech Republic, by Toma Bat'a whose family had been shoe makers for generations.

HIGH STREET, DEAL.

G.1932.

A variety of sunblinds adorn Deal High Street in the 1930s – a scene that would be devastated by bombing in 1940. In the centre of this view is the 'Pianos' sign of Goulden and Wind's music shop. AJ Harris Mayes has its butcher's premises at number 44. The International Stores was next door at 46-48. The clock of Claude Darracott jewellers, later Simmonds, and a second clock further along at Hunnisett's drapery stand at 4.10pm.

At about 10.30am on Friday 11 October 1940, a busy shopping morning, four high explosive bombs were dropped on the High Street. They demolished the Westminster Bank alongside The Black Horse Hotel, right, and the living accommodation above Goulden and Wind's music and piano shop. Both gas and water mains in the High Street were ruptured. Amazingly, only four people were injured.

Fleming Reid and Company's Scotch Wool and Hosiery Stores were based in Greenock, in the early 1900s and had branches throughout the country, including at 54 High Street, Deal, as early as 1913. When this shop front was pictured by Basil Kidd, probably in the early 1960s, it was a modern design but is now a reminder of more traditional facades. At the bottom of the left hand window ladies' nylon briefs are on sale for 4/9d a pair.

Inside the Scotch Wool Shop the well turned out staff pose for another Basil Kidd publicity picture. It recalls the luxury, and then standard practice, of tidily arranged shelves of wools, knitwear and brown paper parcels awaiting collection – some bought with the pattern and some purchased later when needed. For the uncertain, a small sign on the counter declares: "Our manageress Miss D Smith will be glad to advise you."

Goulden and Wind's position in the HIgh Street was denoted by a large 'piano' sign at first floor level of the building. In earlier times a lending library was at the rear of the shop. After the Second World War it became the record department. The firm opened in 1903 having taken over from FH Brown.

Goulden and Wind's rebuilt frontage after the bomb damage. Taken in the early 1950s, the new window is at an angle, set back from the pavement. Among the items on display are some of the first affordable televisions made by Philips, Bush, Pye and Ekco, all on reasonable terms ahead of the Queen's coronation in 1953. The entrance door handle was in the shape of a large treble cleft which was polished every day by one of the assistants.

A glimpse inside Goulden and Wind's music department, probably during the mid 1970s judging by the Abba sheet music on the display rack. Distinctly uncool for today's youngsters perhaps, but in the 1950s and 1960s the shop was the in place for records, including the new 45s; its peg board displays and sound proof booths were highly fashionable at that time. Goulden and Wind was the only shop in Deal to sell HMV records and Noel Coward was a customer when he lived at St Margaret's Bay in the late 1940s.

Charles Lock JP, owner of Goulden and Wind, with his staff marking his retirement and the closure of the firm in 1980.

Thomas Steed Bayley, ironmonger, at 38-40 High Street. An alleyway ran between it and the Black Horse Hotel. Steed Bayley, a prominent local figure, was Mayor of Deal in 1905 and 1919-1923. He also served as President of the Deal and Walmer Chamber of Trade in 1905 and 1911. The town's first telephone exchange was located in Steed Bayley's premises.

Walter & Son's shoe shop, 46-48 High Street, in October 2007, just a few days before its closure. At its peak, the company had stores in several other Kent towns but only the Folkestone branch survived by early 2009. As can be seen by the Clark's shop next door, competition was never far away. Walter & Son's Deal branch had previously been the International Tea Company Stores Limited.

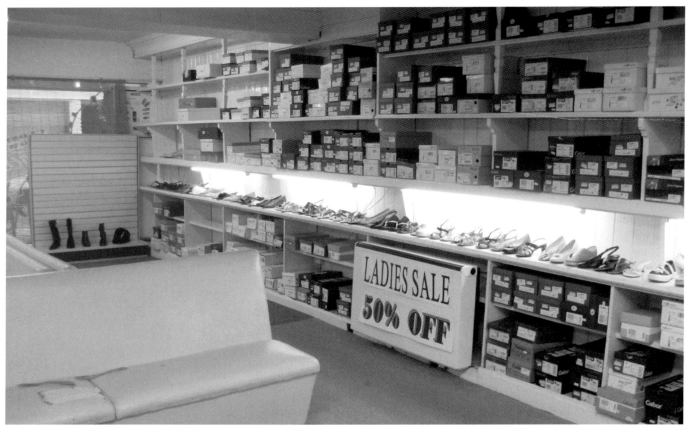

An internal view of Walter & Son during its closing down sale. Daniel Walter started the firm in Hythe in 1849 and at its height had eight branches. Walter & Son first came to Deal in 1956 opening in Brown and Phillips' Queen Street store but later moved to its own High Street premises to take advantage of a better trading position.

Deal High Street as seen in the 1950s with, from the left, Brown and Phillips' furniture store, Vye & Son, the Deal and District Co-operative Society, John Pittock outfitters and Lipton's store on the corner of Park Street where a Morris J delivery van is unloading. On the right of this view can be seen a sign for Harris Mayes meats.

Left: Staff of the provisions section of Vye's around 1946. Back left is Barbara Gaunt, nee Redsull; Peter, a temporary manager and Jill Wellard, nee Holbourn. Front left, Barbara Hunt, nee Staples; Betty Blanche, nee Smith and Sheila Hyatt, nee Wells. Right: Staff from the bacon and cheese section of the store were, from left, Mary Minter, nee Files; Bill Gladwish and Margaret Trice. In front is possibly John Nadin, or George Ballard of Sandwich.

Left: These are the imposing premises of John Pittock and Son, drapers and outfitters, as seen in the late 1800s at 49–53 High Street. The firm, which finally closed in 1978, could claim a proud history dating from at least 1628 when glover and hosier William Pittock took over a small shop in Lower Street. Pittock & Son became the longest running business in Deal and, according to trade magazine The Outfitter, probably in the country.

Below: John Pittock in 1957 when he became a magistrate.

MANTLE & MILLINERY SHOWROOM

The ladies mantles and millinery showrooms of John Pittock from the early 1900s. At the height of the Edwardian era in 1909 the firm announced the opening of a new department for these goods, promising 'A day of interest for every lady in Deal'. Advertisements described costumes of 'Venetian cloth, lined with striped Glisade and Italian pleated skirt' and 'chic gowns of French cashmere'.

A more recent internal view of John Pittock outfitters taken in 1957 showing the office on the left – all box files and filing cabinets – and the stairs to the first floor department where school uniforms and ladies' fashions were sold. Men's shirts and jackets are visible on the right of the photo.

John Pittock stands outside the family shop which became Gieves & Hawkes, of London's Savile Row, when he retired in 1978. Mr Pittock took over in 1936 from his father Sidney, a town Alderman, and was the twelfth member of the family to run the business. The shop stayed open during both world wars – during the second Mrs Pittock ran the business after her husband joined the RAF.

Brown & Phillips furniture store, at 43 High Street, was next to Marks and Spencer. Furniture and carpets were on the first floor with curtain fabric and bedding. A china and glass department was in the basement. In 2006 M&Co sought permission to make major alterations. In 2003 Brown and Phillips fashion shop closed at 62-64 High Street, ending its association with the town which began in 1938 when Mr Vivyan Phillips bought Brown's drapers.

An unusual view of 43 High Street, now a branch of M&Co, taken from the side and rear as building work neared completion. Sidney Pittock, owner of John Pittock's drapers and outfitters, built the shop on the site of Henry Dunn's auction house, which had earlier been the town's playhouse. In 1946 Vivyan Phillips, owner of Brown and Phillips, purchased the shop on Mr Pittock's retirement.

Staff of Brown and Phillips department stores gather round for a photocall during their staff fancy dress party at the Astor Theatre in 1948. On the stage is the band and, no doubt, the MC for the evening. Inset: On the left at the same event, Georgina Curling, nee Harnett, and Kathleen Frater, nee Parker, as Buttons and Bows.

HIGH STREET, DEAL.

D331

A 1950s view of Deal High Street, with Northey's, now Roper's stationers, on the right. Riceman's department store on the left stands where Boots the Chemist is now. Fred Riceman visited Deal on a cold rainy day in January 1950 with a view to buying Clarabutt's, another local store, but wasn't impressed. Luckily, he returned for a second look and Riceman's was born.

Marks and Spencer opened in Deal in July 1937 and this is a photo of a staff party from the 1950s, in the days when stores had much larger numbers of staff. In the centre of the photo is branch manager Mr Owen and, to his right, is deputy Mrs Cluer who later took over from him.

Baz was there! – Basil Kidd, photographer for the East Kent Mercury for many years, captured the last moments of Riceman's window displays and the sad end of a much loved and greatly missed department store as fire takes hold on Sunday 6 October 1963.

Another photo by Basil Kidd as the Riceman's fire takes hold. The blaze threatened neighbouring properties including Hepworth's outfitters and, on the far side, Marks and Spencer.

A welcome awaits you

AT **Ricemans**

DEAL'S DEPARTMENTAL STORE

At RICEMANS, where there are 58 departments under one roof, visitors and residents alike are always welcome to walk around without obligation

RICEMANS RESTAURANT

for **MORNING COFFEES**

LUNCHEONS

AFTERNOON TEAS

and **FRIDAY NIGHT SUPPERS**

The hairdressing salon is at the service of all holidaymakers

Left: Unsurprisingly, the Riceman's fire was front page news in the East Kent Mercury of 10 October 1963. In the story's main picture, Fred Riceman and daughter Elizabeth look on helplessly as the flames take hold. Later, there was much resentment when the firm decided not to rebuild in Deal. Right: A 1959 advert boasts the store's 58 departments including a restaurant and hairdresser – at the service of all holidaymakers.

INTERNATIONAL STORES

The smart, new, trend setting International Stores frontage was captured by Basil Kidd in another publicity shot. International had been across the road at 48 High Street but transferred to Riceman's former site after the 1963 fire. Special offers at the time included Prince's red salmon at 3/10d a tin, New Zealand cheddar for 2/10d per pound while Suncrush orange squash was 1/11d a bottle. The store stayed open until 7.30pm on Fridays.

Although Selwyn's, which became Victor Value, had adapted to become one of the first self service grocery shops along the High Street in the 1950s, it was the new International Stores which was custom designed as self service. Wandering around with a shopping trolley and choosing goods was a novelty although, soon after, the resulting invention of the checkout queue was less welcome!

The cooked meats and dairy sections of International Stores are now part of Boots the Chemist. Prices were still in pre-decimal 'old money' and an opening offer in 1964 included a free tin of processed peas with every pack of own brand sausages! Boots moved in alongside International around the same time, taking over another part of the former Riceman's store, and later extended into International's premises as well.

Martin's newsagent and confectioner occupied the corner of Broad Street and High Street until it closed in December 2008. Staff placed notices in the windows thanking customers for their support while another message read 'Thank you for watching over us CCTV'. Martin's was previously a branch of Colin Beckley's Sweetmarket which in turn had once been Timothy White's.

On the opposite corner to Timothy White's – absorbed into the Boot's the chemist chain in 1968 – was Burton's tailors, yet another name gone from the town's High Street. In this pre Second World war view, a lone policeman stands on the corner by Timothy White's, eyeing the camera with some suspicion. Thompson's Walmer ales and stout were celebrated at regular intervals in the New Inn pub on the left.

Ainslie Brothers butchers' Christmas display celebrates the locally reared prize winning meat, some proclaiming 'Bred by Lord Northbourne'. The shop was at 20 High Street, now a card shop, on the corner of South Court. Alongside can be glimpsed a branch of the Home and Colonial grocery stores and across the road was William Darracott's drapers.

Henry Jarvist Bing astride an Ainslie Brothers butchers' delivery cart.

Woolworth's opened in Deal in 1923 but is pictured here in its final days of trading in January 2009 before the entire company went into administration. Thousands of jobs were lost nationally as hundreds of stores shut down. Inset: The store looking empty and bereft even just a few minutes after closing on 3 January.

Deal's Woolworth's staff pose for the East Kent Mercury during the final day's business. Many of them had been loyal employees for several years but faced immediate redundancy as soon as they had finished packing up the remaining stock and fittings. Before the company took over the premises in the 1920s the building had been the County and Colonial Bank.

This photograph of one of several second floor rooms was taken a few weeks after Woolworth's High Street store closed. Forming part of the County and Colonial Bank's living accommodation, it was occupied in 1911 by the manager Frederick Wilson, his wife Evelyn, who came from Suffolk, their two sons and servant Alice Lockwood. The rooms had remained largely unaltered from when Woolworth's first moved in nearly 90 years ago.

All stock reduced! Store closing! Everything must go! Big, brash red and yellow signs became sadly familiar as the shelves emptied during Woolworth's final closing down sales across the country. The Deal branch was no exception.

One of the many pictures of flooding in this part of town which had been a constant problem for businesses from as far back as the 1800s and persisted until the 1970s when the drainage system was finally upgraded. On the right is Orchard's shoe shop, which was next to Woolworth's. Opposite was Comfort's Ironmongers that had moved from 90 High Street after Second World War bombing and later moved to Queen Street, now the premises of Lynda's Drugstore.

Left: Nicky Orchard, aged five, outside the family's shoeshop that retailed beside Woolworth's. It became John's Menswear and is now a branch of Specsavers. The business had previously been RG Long & Sons boot and shoemakers, with a further shop directly across the street. Right: Maurice Orchard who, with his wife Peggy, owned Orchard's shoe shop. Maurice took over the firm from his father, Malcolm Herbert Orchard who, in turn, had inherited the business from his father Frederick Herbert Orchard.

From 1971, this row of businesses opposite Woolworth's includes Bateman's opticians, Ashley Brown's jewellers and further along, Ferris the butcher. On the left, a Blue Bird toffee van delivers to the tobacconist and sweet shop run by Audrey Todd. Inset: Ashley George Brown the jeweller in the early 1970s.

An Edwardian view from South Street of the High Street shows Lloyd's Bank on the right and next door refreshment rooms selling teas, coffee, cream ices and other treats. By 1911 Swiss confectioner and pastry cook Pietro Antonio Codiferro was in business here. The sign for RG Long and Son, boot and shoemakers, is clearly visible. Opposite here is draper Fred Franklin. The gates of the County and Colonial Bank can just be seen beyond.

An ornate bill heading dated 1895 for Clifton Brothers, grocers of 5-7 High Street. In Memories of Deal, Mrs Kate Parker wrote the two brothers were 'each wearing a black velvet cap (with) all flowers worked round them'. One brother 'took a piece of blue paper from the shelf … he wound it round his hand and screwed up the bottom. He poured tea in it and sugar and coffee in others'.

Apparently this wasn't the first time an East Kent bus tried to demolish King's gift and toy shop when leaving the nearby depot in South Street in the 1960s. This Basil Kidd shot captures a close up of the shop which had moved to 1 High Street, at the corner of Wellington Road, from 88 High Street, after being bombed during the Second World War. The firm was properly known as AW King and Son Limited, the owner being Sir Alexander William King who succeeded to a baronetcy in 1954 when his uncle died. His son Sir Peter King ran the business until his death in 1973 and it was finally sold in 1980. For enthusiasts, the bus was a 1957 registered Guy Arab Mark IV with Park Royal body and survived with East Kent until sold on in 1971.

Victoria Road – Early morning and the assistant unfurls the blind at the beginning of the day's trading. The shop stands on the corner of South Street and Victoria Road but in the mid 1800s was known as Prospect Place before demolition of the naval yard and subsequent building of properties in Victoria Town. The shop's name is obscured but John Woodcock was listed as a baker at Prospect Place in 1849. The shop had become Tapping's bakery by 1899 but has now sadly lost its grandure and was standing empty in early 2009.

Left: This grand and ornate illustration for John Tapping's bakery on the corner of Victoria Road and South Street captures the individuality and style of many earlier businesses. John Arthur Tapping began the firm in the late 1800s and expanded with other branches including Walmer and Kingsdown. Mr Tapping's son John, who was Mayor of Deal three times, carried on the business. Both he and his father were Presidents of the Deal and Walmer Chamber of Trade.

Below: A 1931 advert from the local newspaper for Tapping's bread and cakes.

A CERTAINTY !!!

There are few certainties in this world ; but one is the excellent quality and flavour and value of

JOHN TAPPING'S Bread & Cakes.

Always Good Alike.

Shop at
2, VICTORIA ROAD, DEAL. Tel. 87.   18, STRAND, WALMER. Tel. 43.
THE CAKE SHOP, UPPER WALMER.
And our Roundsmen in every Street.

Nicholas Kingsman Ltd.

formerly

J. TAPPING

For door-to-door bread and cake delivery
which covers Deal, Walmer and District

Phone: DEAL 87

MEET FOR *Espresso Coffee* AT OUR
COFFEE HOUSE   SOUTH STREET

SOUTH STREET

HOYLES INTERIORS

e can deliver throughout
he South East & London

SALE 50% OFF   SALE 50% OFF

This photograph of Hoyle's Interiors pine shop was to represent a modern view of Victoria Road but the business closed in 2008, as already difficult trading conditions worsened. The corner property is still remembered as Tapping's bakery which later became a branch of Nicholas Kingsman Ltd in the 1950s. Inset: Kingsman's advertised its door to door deliveries widely in 1958.

From

CHARLES RUSSELL,

Dufferin House, DEAL.

A BRITISH
JAEGER
pure wool
WEAR
DAY &
NIGHT

Robinson's furniture store at 12-16 Victoria Road, on the corner of Sondes Road, which closed in 2008. Earlier the building had been Charles Russell's outfitters and then from the 1950s until the 1980s, it had been a branch of Courts furniture stores. Inset: A business card for Charles Russell's possibly dating from the 1930s.

A view of Victoria Road in 1934 after yet another flood. On the right is Charles Russell's outfitters. Beyond, on the opposite corner of Sondes Road was The Vale Dairy, later to become part of Dola Dairies. On the left of this view was Clarke and Seymour electrical retailer and, in the distance on the corner of Wellington Road, John Gibbons furniture dealers, later to become King's Bazaar toy shop.

Harold Johnson and his wife Jessie stand outside their greengrocery shop in Victoria Road, opposite the junction with Sondes Road. The shop stood back from the road and was previously Clarke and Seymour electrical dealers, pictured on the left of the previous photograph. Mr and Mrs Johnson moved to Deal in 1945 to open the shop which they ran until around 1957.

Walmer – A view of the central area of The Strand, between St Saviour's Church and North Barrack Road, taken in the late 1800s. Dominating the scene at Russell Terrace, 28-31 The Strand, was Loyns wholesale and retail cash drapers. To the left is their wines, ales and stouts department, then millinery, costumes and drapery. The firm also offered an extensive range of mourning wear.

An impressive illustration for Loyns wholesale and cash drapers from the end of the 19th century. Early advertisements in the East Kent Mercury from 1889 ran the full depth of the broadsheet page, proclaiming its variety of goods from 'The latest novelties in French and English Millinery Gloves and Pongee Silks for Ball Dresses, Sashes etc and black silks for mourning'.

Left: Harlow's still trades today but under a change of ownership. Jim Harlow originally bought the hardware and ironmonger's shop in 1912 and was joined by his son Eric in 1932. To the right is Loyns grocery department where a large ginger cat would take up residence in the shop window amid the bacon and ham. To the left is The Green Café now a bakery.

Below: Eric and Joan Harlow pictured when they retired in August 1984 from the shop at 27 The Strand. Eric had been involved in the business for an impressive 52 years.

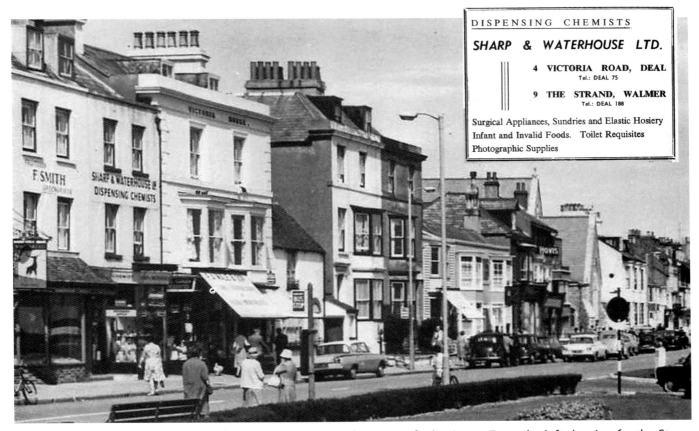

A view of The Strand taken in the early 1960s shows every shop open for business. From the left, the sign for the Stag public house is just visible beside F Smith, fruiterer and greengrocer. Next door, at number 9, was chemist Sharp & Waterhouse which also had a branch at 4 Victoria Road, Deal. Ironmonger PA Wale and Son was alongside – and was still trading in 2009 but under different ownership. Inset: A Sharp & Waterhouse advert from 1956.

An earlier view of The Strand, taken from the Dover Road, in the early 20th century captures the vibrancy of this parade of shops with their ornate verandas and blinds. The 1899 commercial directory gives a flavour of the wide range of businesses within just a few yards of each other: 1 Richard Light, greengrocer; 2 Richard Pittock, butcher; 3 Edward Atkins, decorator; 3a William Murray, tobacconist; and 5 HL Simmons, family grocer.

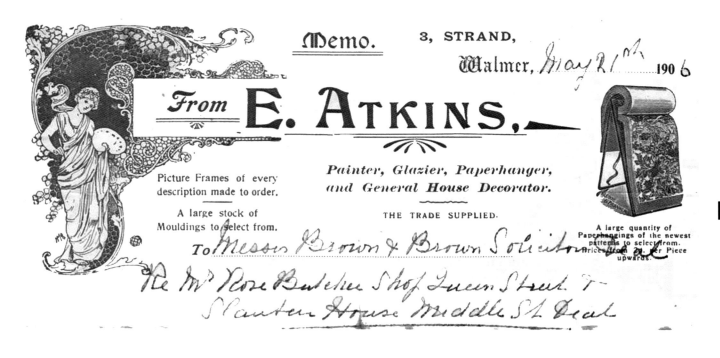

An ornate and artistic bill heading for Edward Atkins, decorator of 3 The Strand, dated 1906, that provides an estimate of £7 15 shillings to Emmerson, Brown and Brown Solicitors for decoration to Mr Rose's butchers in Queen Street, Deal, and their slaughterhouse in Middle Street.

Off Dover Road – Albert George Woodward stands proudly outside his cycle shop at 4 Cambridge Road, Walmer. Mr Woodward was in business from the late 1890s and in one of his many adverts for the Humber Cycle proclaimed: "Lady Wentworth writes: The Beeston Humber is the lightest and most comfortable bicycle I have ever tried." Prices were from £6 6s up to £14 with illustrated catalogue available. Mr Woodward was well known for cycling his trusty penny farthing along the seafront but how he climbed on – and off – remains a mystery!

Reginald George Wilson was an antique dealer, cabinetmaker and upholsterer at 2 and 3 Cambridge Road, Walmer – 'French polishing a speciality and carpets beaten and re-laid'. With his wife Louisa, they also ran a domestic agency from the premises. The shop was to the side of The Cambridge Arms public house and went through to the neighbouring property that is currently Audio Ice. To the left can just be seen Boothby's butcher's shop.

Number 3 Cambridge Road, which still retains its former shop window, was once Louise's gown shop run by Bessie Wilson, sister of RG Wilson of the nearby antique shop.

Below: Pictured in stylish blouse and pearls, Bessie Wilson is remembered by a former customer as a very statuesque lady.

PICKARD,
FAMILY BUTCHER
ENGLISH AND COLONIAL BEST QUALITY.

VILLAGE STREET

W. JAMES, UPPER WALMER.

Defining a bygone age when life was much slower is this late 19th century view of the Dover Road at Upper Walmer. The only vehicle is the cart outside Henry Sackville Pickard's family butcher. In 2009 the premises were still a butcher's shop – run by Graham Johns and his family – retaining the ornamental ironwork for the blinds. Woodcock's general store was next door and Vye's the grocer later had a branch further along the road.

Mill Hill, Deal – This purpose built parade of shops went up in the early 1930s to serve the growing mining community. At 34-36 Mill Hill, now Posh Paws, were Bill Holborn's butchers shop and Mrs Brown's hairdresser, later run by son Les. At number 40 was Alf Brown's cycle shop; he had won the toss for the larger of two shops – his brother Edwin ran the smaller as a shoe shop. Later, Mr Bane took on the cycle shop with his wife Ella taking part of it for haberdashery.

Edwin Brown at the window of his shoe shop at 42 Mill Hill which he opened around 1930. Mr Brown holds a sign for clogs to promote the footwear he made for coal miners and repaired along with other shoes. The business remained in the family as a shoe shop and repairers until its closure in 2002 having later been run by Edwin's son Bob and grandson John.

Bryn Limbrick, in 1958 standing alongside the Austin A30 van he used for deliveries from Bill Holborn's butchers. Bryn had started working for Mr Holborn as errand boy aged 11 while still at school. He remembers delivering meat on his bicycle, pushing the large bike because he was too small to ride it. He continued helping Mr Holborn between shifts as a miner and bought the shop in 1966.

Bryn and Julie Limbrick's butchers shop which they owned for 18 years. They had bought Bill Holborn's premises and Les Brown's barbers next door, to make one bigger shop. Away from work, Les was a first class darts player who would often challenge customers to a game in the shop using six inch nails as his darts. Nine times out of ten he would also have a motorbike in pieces on the shop floor around which customers would have to negotiate!

Corner shops – Young Florence and Bertha Capp stand outside the family sweet shop on the corner of York Road at 1 North Barrack Road in Walmer around 1928. Their parents Walter Benjamin Capp and his wife Florence ran the shop and a coal merchant's business next to the Lord Warden public house.

Left: Robert Strouts and his son Bob at the doorway of the family shop on the corner of Wollaston Road and York Road around 1950. The family moved to Deal from London in 1936 and took over from Charlie Jones. Right: A picture from 1964 with six year old Gary, Bob's son, taking his turn to stand in the doorway of the shop. Bob continued to run the business until 1983.

JC Maund's grocery shop near the corner of Rectory Road at 296 St Richard's Road. John Charles Maund and his wife took over the shop in 1951 in what had been the front room of the house. Mr Maund became a familiar figure delivering groceries to customers on his bicycle. Like many corner shop owners, the couple worked long hours providing an essential service to the local community. Perhaps the tricycle parked on the pavement belongs to a young customer sent on a last minute errand by his or her mother!

Surf washing powder, blocks of kitchen salt, packets of Kellogg's Corn Flakes, Ryvita, Aspirin tablets, Blue Gillette razor blades, jars of sweets and oranges sold loose at five for one shilling are among the variety of post-war goods packed inside JC Maund's small shop. A sign invites customers to join the Christmas club while a set of scales stands sentinel on the counter in this evocative scene.

All traces of the former shop front at 16 London Road, near the fire station, have gone but for many years this was a popular confectioner and tobacconist. Inset left: Herbert Edwin Piddock and his wife Annie Laurie ran it during the 1930s. Herbert was a master tailor, having learnt his trade in the Royal Marines. He used to sit in the room behind the shop carrying out tailoring alterations in between serving customers. Inset right: Frank and Doris Corcoran were in charge during the 1950s and 1960s and also ran a second sweet shop and tobacconists in South Street. They were also a driving force of the League of Friends of Deal Hospital.

May Beerling outside the family shop in Church Lane with youngest son Peter. Her husband Raymond was a market gardener, selling produce from the back door before the front room was turned into a shop. When the Birdwood Avenue estate was built the phrase for many local families was often 'we're going round Beerlings'. Later, the shop became Ron's Emporium – a sprawling, and popular, secondhand shop – but was demolished in 2007 for housing.

Mr and Mrs Beerling with their children Johnny, Vera and baby Peter beside the family home and shop c1950. Johnny grew up to become the controller of BBC Radio One between 1985 and 1993. His distinguished career at the BBC saw him help launch the station in 1967 and create its annual summer roadshow in 1973. Johnny now lives in Yorkshire.

In March 2008 The Trading Post, on the corner of Church Lane and Orchard Avenue, inset, closed after many years and was demolished, apparently yet another corner shop gone. However in summer 2009 a new building with flats and a shop was built – a positive note on which to end this book. Proof the corner shop is not dead and neither, hopefully, is local town shopping.

Bibliography

Country Life magazine (1947) The Threat to Deal, Kent – 29th August 1947

Deal Now and Then (1999) – Deal Town Council

Holyoake, Gregory (1981) Old Deal and Walmer – Meresborough Books

Kelly's Directories, various years including 1899, 1913, 1934

Laker, John (1921) History of Deal – TF Pain & Sons Ltd 2nd edn

Morrison, KA (2007) English Shops and Shopping: An architectural History – Yale University Press

Nunns, Gertrude (2006) A History of Deal – Hovellers Press

Pain, EC (1948) Deal and the Downs in the War of Liberation 1939-1945 – TF Pain and Sons Ltd

Pain, EC Reminiscences of Old Deal – TF Pain and Sons Ltd

Pain, H Deal and Walmer Directory – various years including 1911, 1938, 1956

Parker, K Memories of Deal (c1975) unpublished

Powell, Rowland (2001) 45 Beach Street, Deal – Bygone Kent Vol 22 May 2001 p301-310

Sargent, Andrew (1999) The Life and Times of a Small House in Deal

www.hereshistorykent.org.uk

www.your-family-history.com/o/oatridge-family-history.